Look Inside a
Pond

Louise Spilsbury

Raintree is an imprint of Capstone Global Library Limited, a company incorporated in England and Wales having its registered office at 7 Pilgrim Street, London, EC4V 6LB – Registered company number: 6695582

To contact Raintree please phone 0845 6044371, fax + 44 (0) 1865 312263, or email myorders@raintreepublishers.co.uk. Customers from outside the UK please telephone +44 1865 312262.

Text © Capstone Global Library Limited 2013
First published in hardback in 2013
The moral rights of the proprietor have been asserted.

Edited by Rebecca Rissman, Dan Nunn, and John-Paul Wilkins
Designed by Steve Mead
Original illustrations © Capstone Global Library Ltd 2013
Illustrations by Gary Hanna
Picture research by Ruth Blair
Production by Alison Parsons
Originated by Capstone Global Library Ltd
Printed in China

ISBN 978 1 406 25128 9 (hardback)
16 15 14 13 12
10 9 8 7 6 5 4 3 2 1

British Library Cataloguing in Publication Data
Spilsbury, Louise.
Look inside a pond.
577.6'3-dc23
A full catalogue record for this book is available from the British Library.

Acknowledgements
We would like to thank the following for permission to reproduce photographs: Alamy pp. 14 (© Terry Whittaker), 27 (© FLPA); Corbis p. 28 (© */Design Pics); Naturepl pp. 15, 23 (© Stephen Dalton), 17 (© Frei / ARCO), 20 (© GEOFF DORE), 24 (© Jane Burton), 25 (© Kim Taylor), 26 (© Paul Hobson); Photoshot p. 21 (© NHPA); Shutterstock pp. 5 (© optimarc), 6 (© Elenaphotos21), 7 (© Stargazer), 8 (© Ron Rowan Photography), 9 (© Andreas Altenburger), 11 (© Naas Rautenbach), 12 (© bluecrayola), 13 (© Uryadnikov Sergey), 18 (© Andreas G. Karelias), 19 (© Laurie L. Snidow), 29 (© formiktopus).

Cover photograph of common frog (*Rana temporaria*), also known as the European Common Frog, reproduced with permission of Shutterstock (© Uryadnikov Sergey).

We would like to thank Michael Bright and Diana Bentley for their invaluable help in the preparation of this book.

Every effort has been made to contact copyright holders of any material reproduced in this book. Any omissions will be rectified in subsequent printings if notice is given to the publisher.

Disclaimer
All the internet addresses (URLs) given in this book were valid at the time of going to press. However, due to the dynamic nature of the internet, some addresses may have changed, or sites may have changed or ceased to exist since publication. While the author and publisher regret any inconvenience this may cause readers, no responsibility for any such changes can be accepted by either the author or the publisher.

Contents

Some words are shown
in bold, **like this**. You can
find out what they mean
by looking in the glossary.

At the surface

A pond is a small area of **fresh water**. A pond is a type of **habitat** where some animals find **shelter** or food. Some animals live on or visit the surface of a pond.

Pond skaters are **insects** that can run on water! Their long legs help them to skate on the top of ponds. They use their short front legs to catch small insects to eat.

▲ Tiny hairs on the pond skater's legs stop it from falling through the surface of the water.

A duck is a bird that has **webbed feet** to help it swim. It swims to find plants, snails, frogs, and other small animals to eat. It also sticks its head under water to find food in the mud.

webbed feet

You can tell ▶ this mallard duck is a **male** because it has a green head.

▲ Mother ducks show babies where to find food.

Female ducks make **nests** of grass and feathers near ponds. They lay their eggs inside the nest. The baby ducks that **hatch** out of the eggs can swim straight away.

Dragonflies fly faster than any other **insects**. They can also **hover** in one spot over a pond, like a helicopter. Their huge eyes look all around to find flies and other insects to eat.

▼ This dragonfly is on the lookout for food.

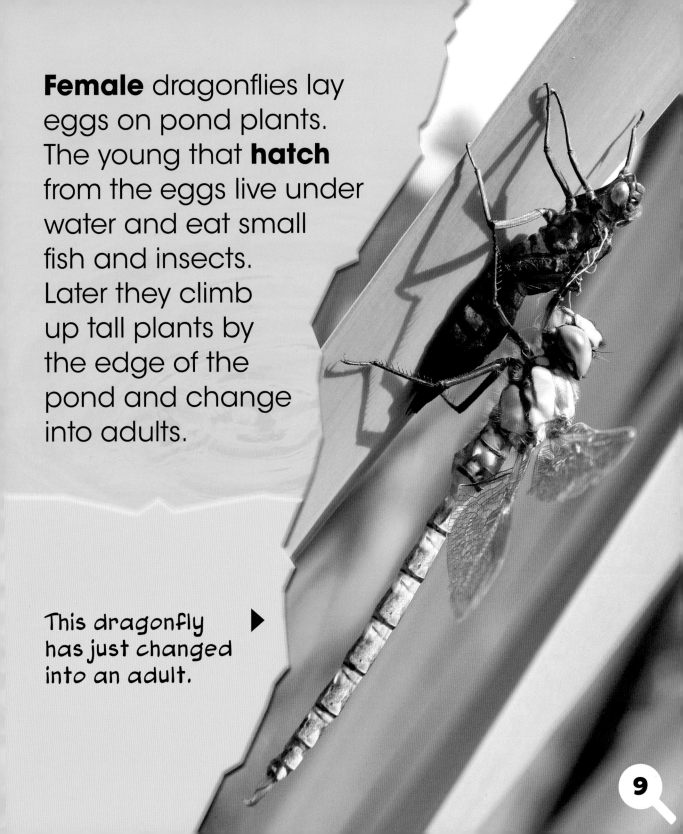

Female dragonflies lay eggs on pond plants. The young that **hatch** from the eggs live under water and eat small fish and insects. Later they climb up tall plants by the edge of the pond and change into adults.

This dragonfly ▶ has just changed into an adult.

On the bank

Some animals live on or in the muddy **bank** next to the pond. Other animals visit the bank to eat the animals that live there.

Herons are grey birds with long legs. They stand very still by the pond and watch for food. Herons stab the water to catch fish and frogs in their beaks.

▲ A long, sharp beak is great for catching fish!

Frogs are **amphibians**. They live on land but lay their eggs in water. **Tadpoles** that **hatch** from the eggs have tails to swim. They live and feed on plants under water.

▼ These tadpoles have recently hatched.

▲ This adult frog is fully grown.

Tadpoles grow into frogs. Their tails shrink and they grow legs so they can hop out of the pond. Frogs catch flies and other small animals to eat on the pond edge using their long, sticky tongues.

Water shrews dig short tunnels into the **bank**. They make warm **nests** inside for their babies from leaves and sticks. Water shrews hide in tunnels to escape birds and fish that try to eat them!

▼ Water shrews are about as long as a pencil.

▲ Big, hairy feet help water shrews to dive.

Water shrews leave their tunnels to dive for food. The stiff hairs that cover their back feet help them to swim. They catch pond **insects** and small fish using their sharp, pointy teeth.

In the water

Some animals live under water in the pond for most or all of the time. They swim about and catch all the food they need in the water.

Pike are big, fierce fish with sharp teeth. They hide among pond plants and dart out quickly to catch **prey** that swims past. Pike eat fish, frogs, ducklings, and water shrews.

▲ Big eyes help pike to spot prey!

Terrapins are small turtles that live in ponds. They kick their **webbed feet** to swim about. Terrapins have a hard mouth like a beak that snaps up fish, plants, and **tadpoles**.

▼ Terrapins can eat and sleep under water.

▲ Terrapins like to warm up in the sun.

Terrapins can stay in the water for days but they often climb out on to rocks or logs to warm up in the sunlight. If there is not much space they may lie on top of each other! Terrapins also lay their eggs on land.

The diving beetle spends most of its time under water. It comes to the surface to collect air bubbles under its wing covers. It uses this air to breathe when it dives and swims.

▼ Diving beetles are great swimmers.

▲ This diving beetle is munching a tadpole.

Diving beetles dart quickly through water looking for food. They move their hairy back legs like paddles to swim along. The beetles have large **jaws** to catch and eat fish and **tadpoles**.

Muddy bottom

The bottom of a pond can be muddy and dark. It is a good place to hide from **predators** and to lay eggs.

Caddis fly eggs **hatch** under water. The young caddis flies are like little caterpillars. They make cases around themselves from sand, shells, and bits of plant. The cases protect their soft bodies.

▲ A case of shells is a safe place to hide!

Small stickleback fish have sharp spines sticking up on their backs. These make it hard for herons, water shrews, and other **predators** to swallow them! Sticklebacks eat worms, **insects**, eggs, and small fish.

▼ Sticklebacks are a tricky meal for many fish!

spine

▲ The male makes a nest from plants and stones.

Male sticklebacks make **nests** at the bottom of the pond. The **female** lays eggs inside the nest. The male chases off any animals that try to eat the eggs.

Crayfish hide under stones in the day and creep out at night to catch food. Crayfish have ten legs for walking quickly across a pond floor.

▼ Crayfish have tough shells and big claws.

claw

fish

▲ Crayfish are not fussy eaters!

Crayfish use their giant claws to catch and hold food. They eat snails, **insects**, fish, eggs, and almost anything else they can find on the muddy bottom!

Pond habitats

In summer, pond water is warm and there are many plants. Many animals are in the pond. In winter, ponds are cold and there are fewer plants. Fewer animals are in the pond.

▼ A pond in summer.

▲ A pond in winter.

Ponds are great places to spot animals.
Sit and watch them come and go, but
remember:
- Even shallow water can be dangerous,
  so take care near the edge of a pond.
- Do not remove plants or animals from
  ponds because they may not survive
  away from them.

Glossary

amphibian type of animal that begins life in water and then lives on land for part of its life. Newts, frogs, and toads are types of amphibian.

bank ground at the edge of a river or stream

female sex of an animal or plant that is able to produce eggs or seeds. Females are the opposite sex to males.

fresh water water in rivers, ponds, and many lakes that is not salty like seawater

habitat place where particular types of living things are likely to live. For example, polar bears live in snowy habitats and camels live in desert habitats.

hatch come out of an egg

hover stay hanging in the air

insect type of small animal that has three body parts, six legs, and usually wings. Ants and dragonflies are types of insect.

jaw part of an animal's mouth used to grip, chew, or bite

male sex of an animal or plant that is unable to produce eggs or seeds. Males are the opposite sex to females.

nest place where a bird or other animal lays eggs or cares for its young. Nests are often made from twigs or grass.

predator animal that hunts and catches other animals for food

prey animal that is caught and eaten by another animal

shelter place that provides protection from danger or bad weather

tadpole young stage in a frog's life cycle. Tadpoles live under water before changing into frogs.

webbed feet feet with skin stretched between the toes that animals, such as ducks and frogs, use to help them swim

Find out more

Books

Minibeasts in a Pond (Where to Find Minibeasts),
Sarah Ridley (Franklin Watts, 2010)

Ponds (Nature Trails), Anita Ganeri (Raintree, 2011)

RSPB First Book of Pond Life, Derek Niemann
(A & C Black, 2012)

Websites

Explore pond habitats and do a virtual pond dip at:
**http://www.naturegrid.org.uk/pondexplorer/
pondexplorer.html**

See videos of ponds and lakes and animals that live
in them at:
http://www.bbc.co.uk/nature/habitats/Lake

Discover more about pond life at:
**http://www.enchantedlearning.com/biomes/
pond/pondlife.shtml**

Index